Teddy Bear
Knits

MO SMITH

Teddy Bear Knits

Salem

House

SALEM HOUSE PUBLISHERS

TOPSFIELD, MASSACHUSETTS

Dedication

This book is dedicated to my husband, Ray, and my children, Andrew and Deborah.

It is written in appreciation of the Westminster Hospital and will help support the Andrew Bostic Fund, which was begun to help finance bone marrow transplants.

Thanks go especially to my mother, Kathleen Francis and my sister, Yvonne Gale for all their help with the knitting of the sweaters.

DESIGN: Bridgewater Associates

EDITORIAL: Amy Carroll

MODEL PHOTOGRAPHY: Fiona Pragoff

PHOTOGRAPHY ART DIRECTION: Michele Walker

STILL LIFE PHOTOGRAPHY: Larry Bray

ILLUSTRATION: Katy Sleight

First published in the United States by
Salem House Publishers, 1987,
462 Boston Street, Topsfield, MA 01983
Copyright © 1987 by Dorling Kindersley
Limited
Story and design of garments copyright
© 1987 Mo Smith

Library of Congress Cataloging-in-Publication Data
Smith, Mo, 1948–
Teddy bear knits.
Summary; Brief text and illustrations follow a teddy bear's adventures as
he searches for the rainbow. Each of the illustrations is transformed into a
charted sweater pattern that includes making-up instructions and a
photograph of the finished garment.
1. Sweaters. 2. Knitting – Patterns. 3. Children's clothing. [1. Sweaters.
2. Knitting – Patterns. 3. Teddy bears – Fiction] I. Title.
TT825.S65   1987   746.9'2   87–9773
ISBN 0-88162-280-X

Bear in Mind

This is a knitting book and story book combined. In it are 16 sweater patterns which highlight the key moments in Jed, our hero's, search for the rainbow, and the happiness it represents. I hope that you will enjoy reading the story to your children and making the sweaters, as much as I think your children will enjoy wearing them.

MAKING THE SWEATERS As you read through the book you will notice the sweater designs each have a separate pattern chart; these either precede or follow the story.

A *"bear essentials"* box gives specific instructions for each design – the colors used in ribs, sleeves, neckband and back; notes on special embroidery; the yarns used, plus a chart giving numbers of balls for the different sizes; and a selection of appropriate buttons.

● The sweaters feature two different necklines – a crew neck and a boat neck – basic instructions for both styles are given on page 63. All the sweaters have been designed using Knitting Worsted. Any brand that uses no. 5 (4mm) needles and works to a tension of 12 stitches and 15 rows to 2 inches (5cm) using stockinette stitch will be suitable. Use the yarn swatches with each design to match up the colors.

● The sweater sizes given are expressed in inches and should be the child's actual chest measurement. The finished garments will knit up slightly larger.

● For beginners, or those whose skills are rusty, a basic knitting ted-niques section (see pp.54–62), illustrates everything you need to know to successfully knit up the sweaters.

● One further note – Jed's eyes are safety ones – they have a "lockable" back which makes it practically impossible for them to be removed. Also I've included an extra knitted backing as an added safety measure. However, if you prefer, the eyes can be embroidered as shown in the basic instructions, and of course, the buttons are purely optional.

Bear Beginnings

Jed awoke with a start to the sound of raindrops on the window. It had been raining for some time and the sun was just peeping through the clouds. Suddenly he became aware of a beautiful curve of color stretched right across the sky. Red, orange, yellow, green, blue, purple, violet — the separate shades gleamed against one another. They began just behind the house opposite and disappeared into a cloud.

"Is this a rainbow?" he wondered. "And what does it look like close up?" Suddenly he made up his mind. He'd go in search of the rainbow.

◆ BEAR ESSENTIALS ◆

Lower ribbing Tweedy Pink
Sleeves Continue in Tweedy Pink until sleeve measures 6½ (7½, 8½, 10, 12)in, 17 (19, 22, 25, 30)cm. Work 4 rows in Bright Pink, 2 rows Bright Blue 4 rows Bright Pink. Change to Cream and work to required length.
Back As chart omitting bear and bed.
Neckband Cream
Embroidery Using Black, work small single stitches for the small teddy's eyes and ears, two stitches for his nose and a longer line for his mouth. Using Bright Blue, work his paws and leg divides in backstitch, and a bow on his neck in satin stitch. Sew two buttons on neck ribbing if desired.

Number of Knitting Worsted 2oz balls per size					
Shade	Size in inches				
	22	24	26	28	30
A Tweedy pink	2	2	2	3	3
B Cream	2	2	3	3	3
C Dark chocolate	1	1	1	1	1
D Warm brown	1	1	1	1	1
E Bright blue	1	1	1	1	1
F Bright pink	1	1	1	1	1
G Yellow	small quantity				
H Black	scrap				

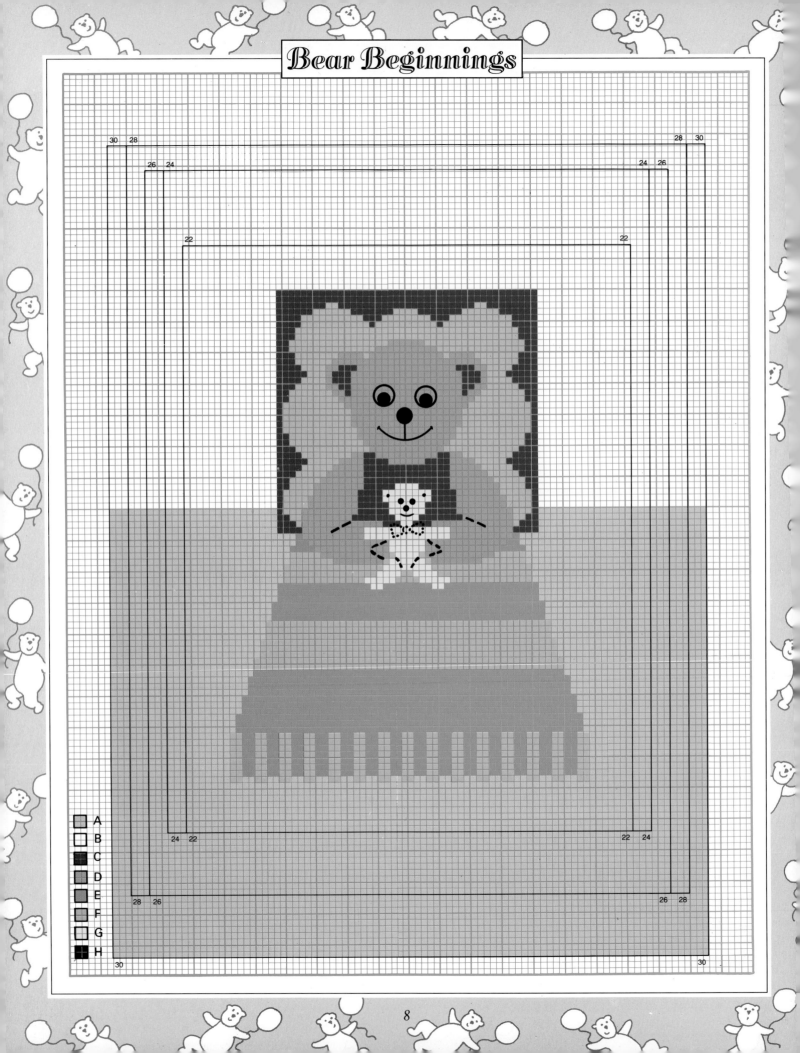

A
B
C
D
E
F
G
H

30 28
26 24
22
28 30
24 26
22

24 22
22 24

28 26
26 28

30
30

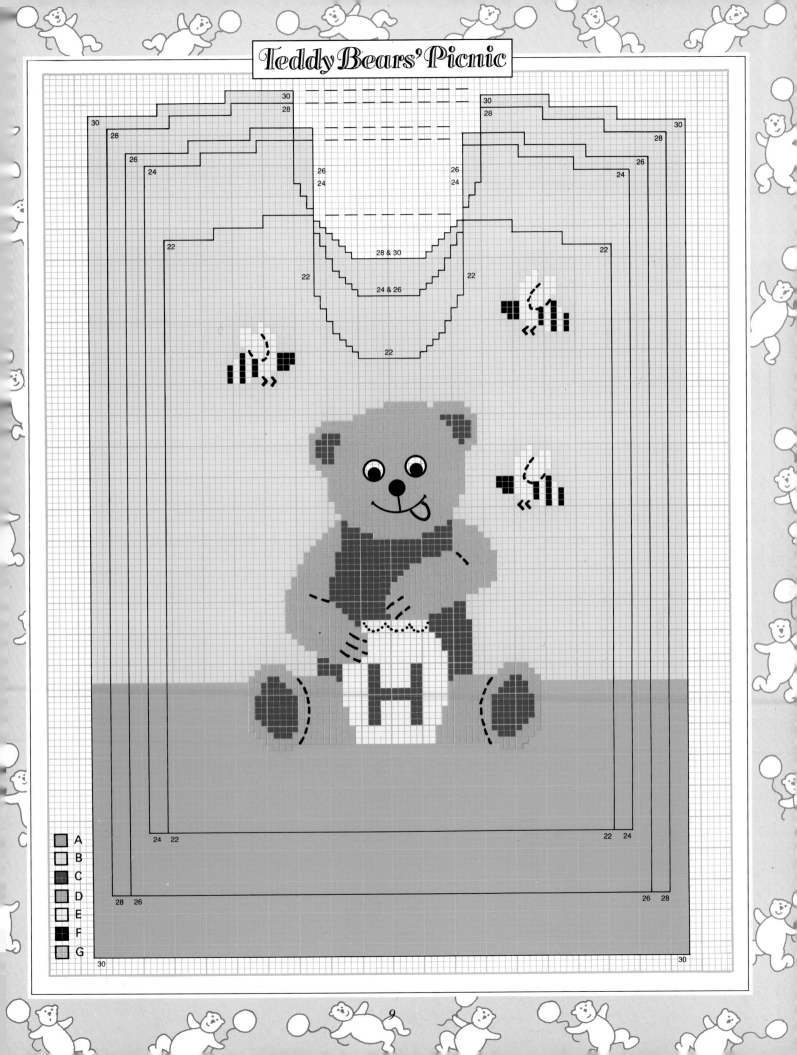

Teddy Bears' Picnic

Jed had never left the house on his own before but he managed to squeeze out through the open window and slide down the drainpipe. He skipped down the path and stopped at the curb. There was nothing coming so he marched bravely across the road and knocked on the door of the house opposite.

"Come in, the door's open." Another bear stood there. Jed told him he wanted to see the rainbow close up. The bear took him through to the garden but the rainbow seemed a million miles away. Jed looked so sad that his friend invited him to a picnic. Jed opened a honey pot and soon began to feel better.

◆ BEAR ESSENTIALS ◆

Lower ribbing Jade green
Sleeves Continue in Jade green until sleeve measures 4¾ (4¾, 6, 6, 7¼)in, 12 (12, 15, 15, 18.5)cm. Change to Light blue and work to required length.
Back As chart omitting teddy and bees.
Neckband Light blue
Embroidery Using Black and backstitch, embroider a wavy line across the top of the honey pot, around the bees' wings and add two legs to each bee. Work teddy's tongue in Bright pink and satin stitch. Use single stitches of Yellow for the bees' eyes. Sew two buttons on shoulder if desired.

Number of Knitting Worsted 2oz balls per size					
Shade	Size in inches				
	22	24	26	28	30
A Jade green	1	2	2	2	3
B Light blue	2	3	3	3	3
C Dark chocolate	1	1	1	1	1
D Warm brown	1	1	1	1	1
E Yellow	small quantity				
F Black	scrap				
G Bright pink	scrap				

The Teddy's Tale

Jed's new friend said he had a special story to tell. "A long time ago, before we belonged to girls and boys, rain came and flooded all the earth. But Noah built an ark and saved two of every kind of animal, including bears. At last, when the rain stopped, Noah opened the doors and shutters of the ark and a beautiful rainbow appeared in the sky. Noah told the animals: "This is a sign that the earth will never be flooded again. From now on, love will be with you always when the sun is shining, and also when it is raining, when you are happy or when you are sad, the rainbow will be there."

◆ BEAR ESSENTIALS ◆

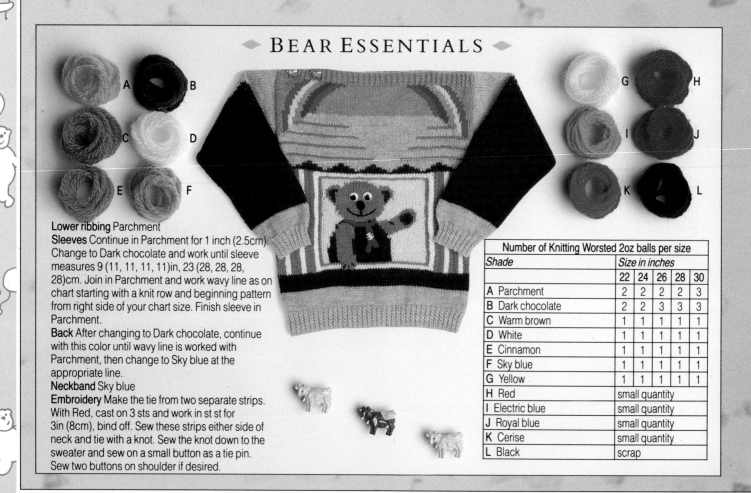

Lower ribbing Parchment
Sleeves Continue in Parchment for 1 inch (2.5cm). Change to Dark chocolate and work until sleeve measures 9 (11, 11, 11, 11)in, 23 (28, 28, 28, 28)cm. Join in Parchment and work wavy line as on chart starting with a knit row and beginning pattern from right side of your chart size. Finish sleeve in Parchment.
Back After changing to Dark chocolate, continue with this color until wavy line is worked with Parchment, then change to Sky blue at the appropriate line.
Neckband Sky blue
Embroidery Make the tie from two separate strips. With Red, cast on 3 sts and work in st st for 3in (8cm), bind off. Sew these strips either side of neck and tie with a knot. Sew the knot down to the sweater and sew on a small button as a tie pin. Sew two buttons on shoulder if desired.

Number of Knitting Worsted 2oz balls per size					
Shade	Size in inches				
	22	24	26	28	30
A Parchment	2	2	2	2	3
B Dark chocolate	2	2	3	3	3
C Warm brown	1	1	1	1	1
D White	1	1	1	1	1
E Cinnamon	1	1	1	1	1
F Sky blue	1	1	1	1	1
G Yellow	1	1	1	1	1
H Red	small quantity				
I Electric blue	small quantity				
J Royal blue	small quantity				
K Cerise	small quantity				
L Black	scrap				

Automobear

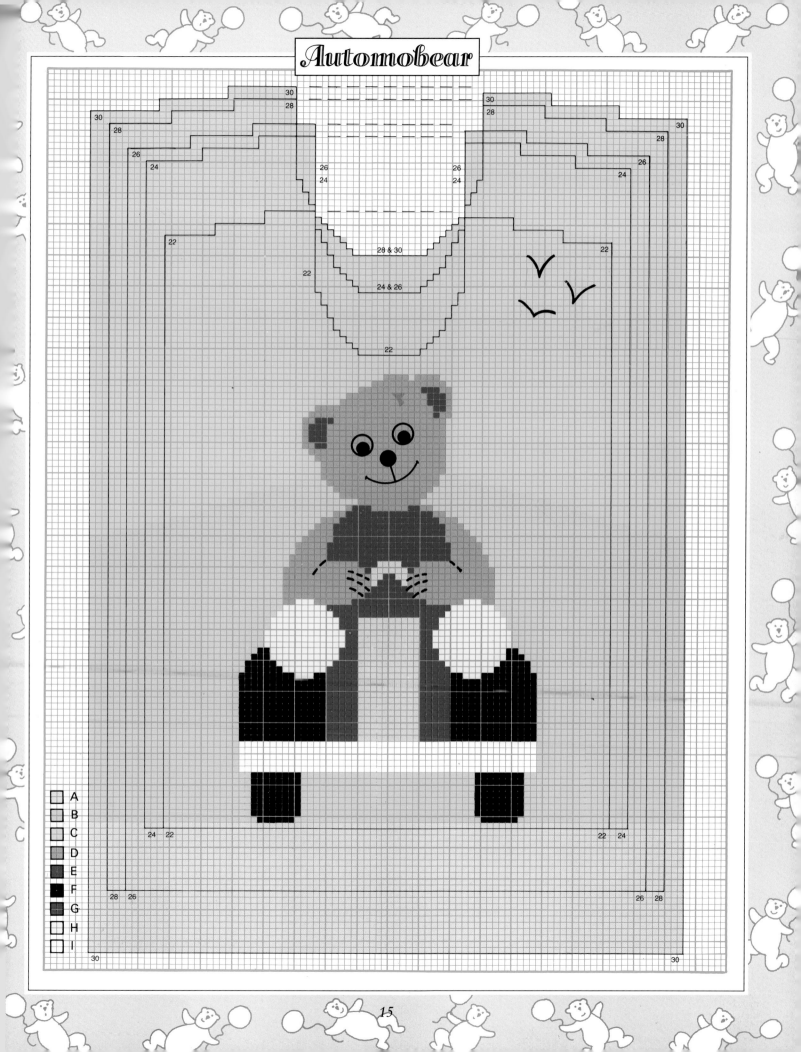

Automobear

Jed liked this story and wanted even more to see the rainbow close up. He began to run and jump, as much as his little legs would let him. Soon he was out of breath. The honey in his tummy was going up and down and he felt sick! Poor teddy. Puffing and panting he came to a lane and saw a little motor car. He climbed in, sounded the horn and began to chug down the road.

It was a beautiful day. The grass looked fresh and green and the buttercups were a bright splash of yellow. In the distance, Jed could see a large striped tent.

◆ BEAR ESSENTIALS

Lower ribbing Chalky gray
Sleeves Change to Pale green after the ribbing and continue until sleeve measures 6½ (6½, 7, 7, 8½)in, 17 (17, 18, 18, 22)cm. Change to Light blue and work to required length.
Back Change to Pale green after the ribbing. Where the first stitches in your size change to Light blue, work straight across in Light blue. Complete back in Light blue.
Neckband Chalky gray
Embroidery Using Black and backstitch, work three birds in the sky. Sew two buttons on shoulder if required.

Number of Knitting Worsted 2oz balls per size					
Shade	Size in inches				
	22	24	26	28	30
A Chalky gray	1	1	1	1	1
B Pale green	2	2	2	3	3
C Light blue	2	2	2	3	3
D Warm brown	1	1	1	1	1
E Dark chocolate	small quantity				
F Black	small quantity				
G Red	small quantity				
H Yellow	small quantity				
I White	small quantity				

Performing Bear

It was a circus! But Jed had no money.
What could he do to get inside? Perhaps
the pair of bears in sparkling leotards
could help. Jed told them his problem.
They whispered together then turned and said:
"You're a bear who's on the ball,
No need to mention money at all,
Entertain us, if you please,
And you'll earn your way with ease!"
And they were as good as their words! Soon Jed
was juggling for joy — tossing balls in the air as
though he were a bear without a care in the world.

◆ BEAR ESSENTIALS ◆

Lower ribbing Tweedy gray
Sleeves Continue in Tweedy gray until sleeve
measures 4 (4, 5, 5, 6)in, 10 (10, 13, 13, 15)cm.
Change to Red and work stripe with Yellow stars as
on chart, working three stars with the center of the
middle star in the center of sleeve. On completion
of stripe change to Yellow. Continue until sleeve is
required length.
Back As chart omitting teddy and balls.
Neckband Red
Embroidery Sew two buttons on teddy and two on
neck ribbing if desired.

Number of Knitting Worsted 2oz balls per size					
Shade	Size in inches				
	22	24	26	28	30
A Tweedy gray	1	2	2	2	2
B Red	1	1	1	1	1
C Yellow	2	2	2	3	3
D Dark chocolate	1	1	1	1	1
E Warm brown	1	1	1	1	1
F Black	scrap				

	A
	B
	C
	D
	E
	F

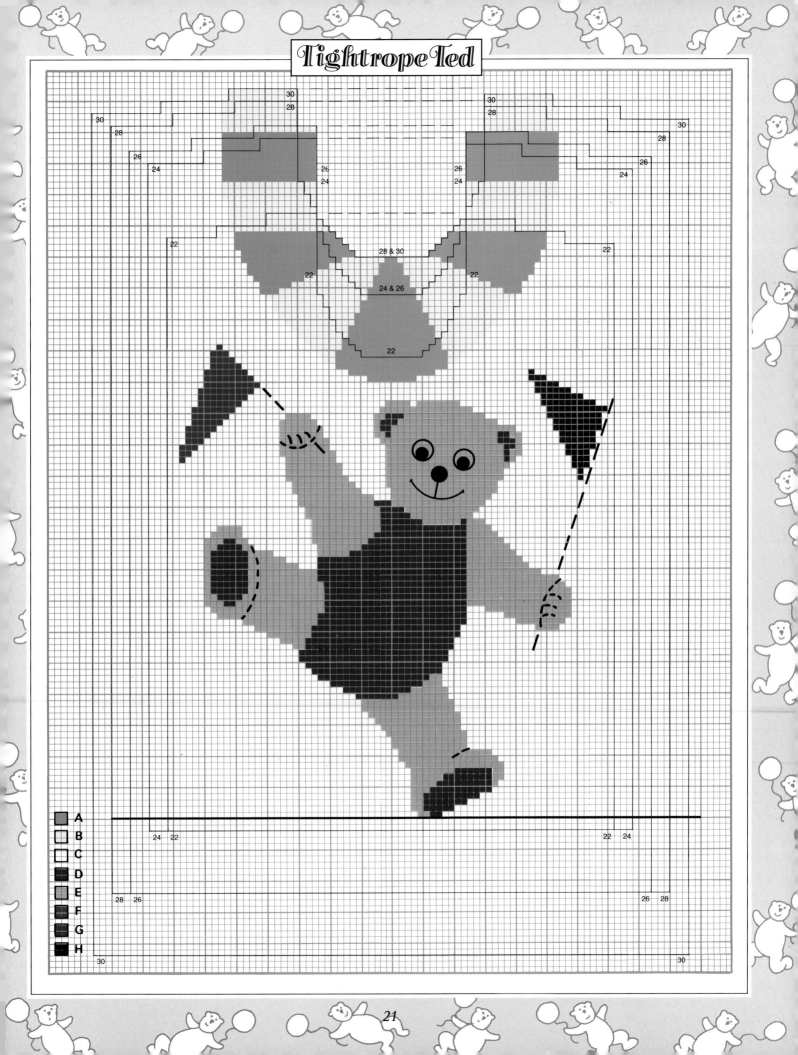

Tightrope Ted

Tightrope Ted

Now Jed couldn't wait to see the performance. He paid with a pocketful of pennies and found a seat inside. The spotlight was on a monkey dressed in a glittering tutu. She climbed a ladder and began to walk the tightrope. Jed jumped out of his seat. He walked across the ring to the monkey. The audience applauded, thinking Jed was part of the act, so Jed performed for them. He copied the monkey on the tightrope and waved his banners about.

Suddenly disaster! Jed's legs began to wobble, his head started to spin, he crashed into the safety net. Jed's days as a circus star were over.

◆ BEAR ESSENTIALS ◆

Lower ribbing Cast on with Electric blue. Next row: Join in Yellow and k1, p1 Yellow, *k1b, p1, k1b Electric blue, p1, k1b Yellow, p1, k1b Electric blue, k1b, p1 Yellow, repeat from * to end. Next row: Rib all stitches in the two colors.

Sleeves After ribbing change to Cream and continue until sleeve is 1½in (4cm) less than required length. Work 4 rows in Electric blue, 2 rows in Yellow, 4 rows in Electric blue, complete sleeve in Cream.

Back After working striped ribbing change to Cream and work the entire back in Cream.

Neckband Electric blue

Embroidery Work two lines in Black from the flags to teddy's paws by laying a length of Black on the sweater from the top of the flag and catching it down every ½in (1cm).

Number of Knitting Worsted 2oz balls per size					
Shade	Size in inches				
	22	24	26	28	30
A Electric blue	1	1	1	1	1
B Yellow	1	1	1	1	1
C Cream	3	3	4	5	5
D Dark chocolate	1	1	1	1	1
E Warm brown	1	1	1	1	1
F Royal	small quantity				
G Red	small quantity				
H Black	small quantity				

Bear and Butterflies

But Jed hadn't forgotten the rainbow! He climbed back into the little car and began to move slowly down a hill. "Sput, sput" went the engine. Then silence. The car rolled down the hill and stopped. Jed climbed out wondering what to do. He looked in to the engine, but his paws were too big to do anything!

Suddenly a crowd of butterflies appeared and Jed gave chase. They led him to the woods, whirling round and round. Soon he was lost. He felt miserable and very sorry for himself. *Bump*. A pine cone fell on his head. He looked up at the tall tree. Could he climb it and find his way back?

◆ BEAR ESSENTIALS ◆

Lower ribbing Blue jade
Sleeves Work grass in Blue jade as on chart, beginning on right side line of your size and working across, joining in Tweedy white. Complete sleeve in Tweedy white.
Back As chart omitting teddy and butterflies
Neckband Blue jade
Embroidery Use Black to work the net in chain stitch and backstitch. Sew two buttons on neck rib if required.

Number of Knitting Worsted 2oz balls per size					
Shade	Size in inches				
	22	24	26	28	30
A Blue jade	1	1	1	1	1
B Tweedy white	2	3	3	4	4
C Dark chocolate	1	1	1	1	1
D Warm brown	1	1	1	1	1
E Cerise	1	1	1	1	1
F Black	scrap				

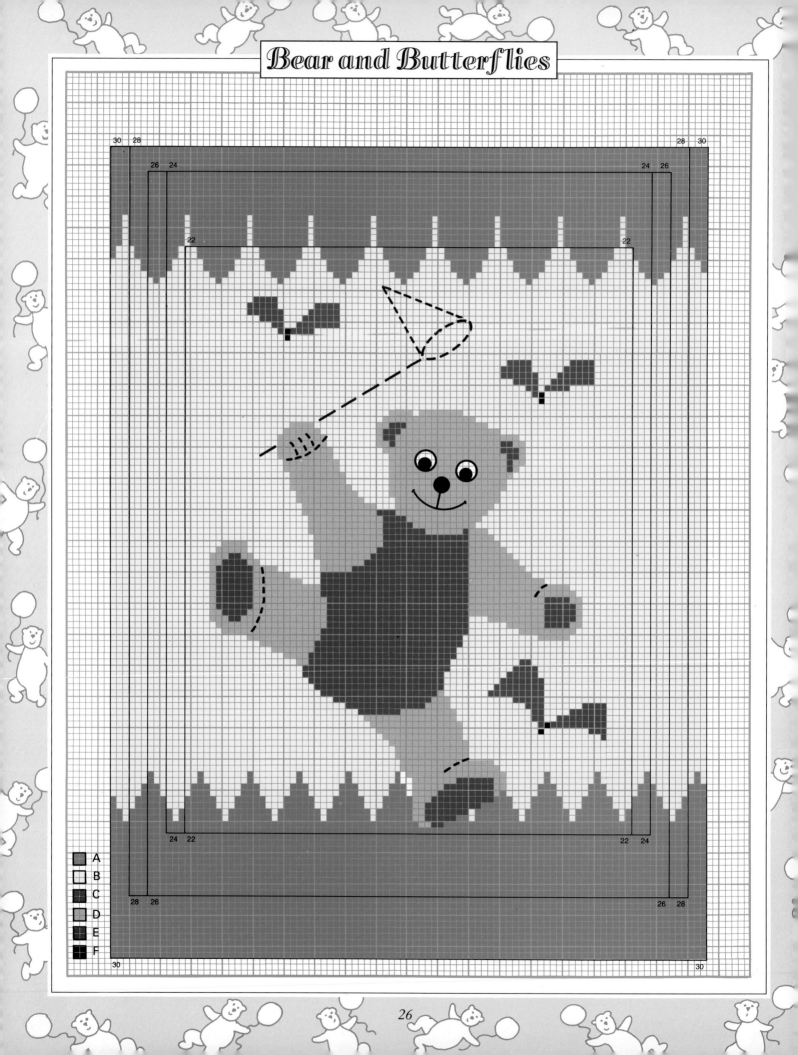

Bear and Butterflies

Unbearable

It was hard for a housebound bear like Jed to climb a tree but at last he reached the top. In the distance he could see the car and below was the path to take. It was a lot harder finding the car than losing it, but at last Jed was back. He reached inside for the umbrella. "This could come in handy," he thought. And it wasn't long before the clouds gathered and it began to rain. Jed stopped for a while under a tree. His feet were wet, but he kept his umbrella up to stop the drips landing on his head.

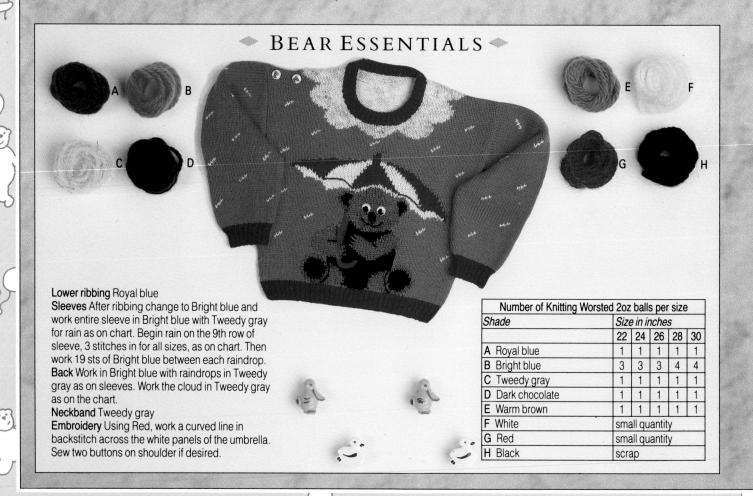

◆ BEAR ESSENTIALS ◆

Lower ribbing Royal blue
Sleeves After ribbing change to Bright blue and work entire sleeve in Bright blue with Tweedy gray for rain as on chart. Begin rain on the 9th row of sleeve, 3 stitches in for all sizes, as on chart. Then work 19 sts of Bright blue between each raindrop.
Back Work in Bright blue with raindrops in Tweedy gray as on sleeves. Work the cloud in Tweedy gray as on the chart.
Neckband Tweedy gray
Embroidery Using Red, work a curved line in backstitch across the white panels of the umbrella. Sew two buttons on shoulder if desired.

Number of Knitting Worsted 2oz balls per size					
Shade	Size in inches				
	22	24	26	28	30
A Royal blue	1	1	1	1	1
B Bright blue	3	3	3	4	4
C Tweedy gray	1	1	1	1	1
D Dark chocolate	1	1	1	1	1
E Warm brown	1	1	1	1	1
F White	small quantity				
G Red	small quantity				
H Black	scrap				

Beach Bear

"To the sea — 5 miles" Jed hadn't known it would take so long when he first set out, but now he was very tired.

At least he was close to a beach. The sea glistened and there was not a cloud in sight. He picked up a towel, pail and shovel and found a quiet spot on the sand.

Jed spent some time building a castle and when it was finished, sat down on his towel to sunbathe. The sun was very hot and he put on his sunglasses. He lay down watching the boats on the horizon wondering where they were going. Before he knew it, he fell fast asleep.

BEAR ESSENTIALS ◆

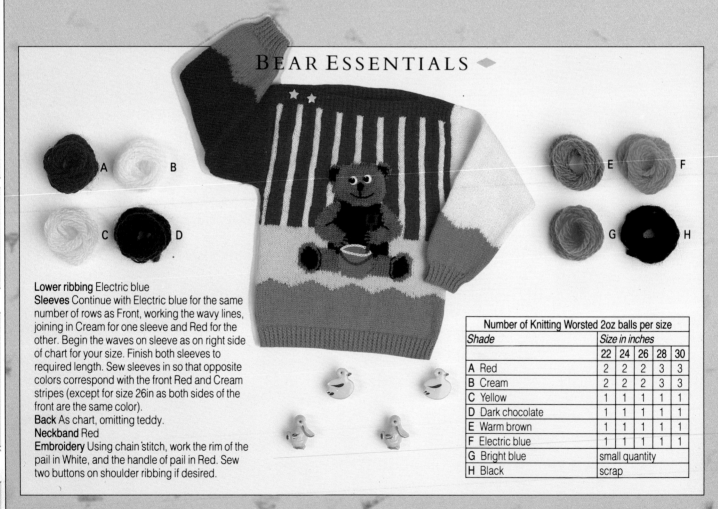

Lower ribbing Electric blue

Sleeves Continue with Electric blue for the same number of rows as Front, working the wavy lines, joining in Cream for one sleeve and Red for the other. Begin the waves on sleeve as on right side of chart for your size. Finish both sleeves to required length. Sew sleeves in so that opposite colors correspond with the front Red and Cream stripes (except for size 26in as both sides of the front are the same color).

Back As chart, omitting teddy.

Neckband Red

Embroidery Using chain stitch, work the rim of the pail in White, and the handle of pail in Red. Sew two buttons on shoulder ribbing if desired.

Number of Knitting Worsted 2oz balls per size					
Shade	Size in inches				
	22	24	26	28	30
A Red	2	2	2	3	3
B Cream	2	2	2	3	3
C Yellow	1	1	1	1	1
D Dark chocolate	1	1	1	1	1
E Warm brown	1	1	1	1	1
F Electric blue	1	1	1	1	1
G Bright blue	small quantity				
H Black	scrap				

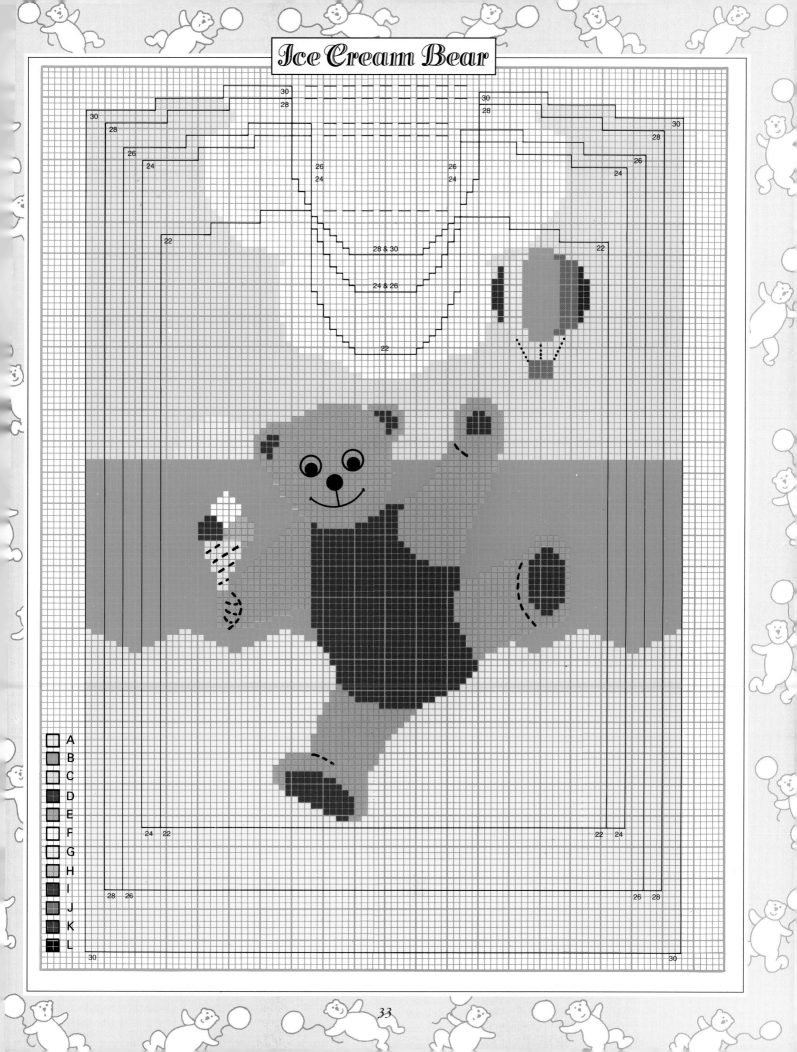

Ice Cream Bear

Ice Cream Bear

Jed awoke with a start. The tide had come in while he was asleep and the water was lapping his toes. He looked around for something else to do and noticed an ice cream van further down the beach.

"This is the life," thought Jed, as he licked a huge cone and felt the coldness sliding down his throat to his tummy. It was delicious. He looked back towards the sea and saw a hot air balloon in the sky. It was the colors of the rainbow. How Jed wished he could have a ride in it. It already had been an exciting day, were there more adventures still to come?

◆ BEAR ESSENTIALS ◆

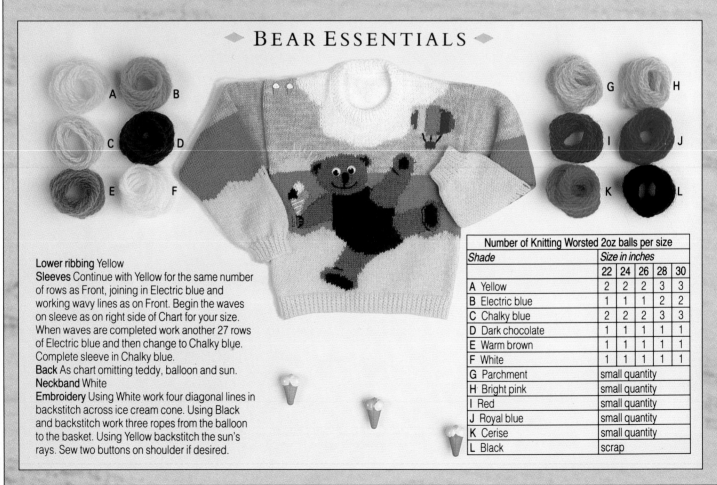

Lower ribbing Yellow
Sleeves Continue with Yellow for the same number of rows as Front, joining in Electric blue and working wavy lines as on Front. Begin the waves on sleeve as on right side of Chart for your size. When waves are completed work another 27 rows of Electric blue and then change to Chalky blue. Complete sleeve in Chalky blue.
Back As chart omitting teddy, balloon and sun.
Neckband White
Embroidery Using White work four diagonal lines in backstitch across ice cream cone. Using Black and backstitch work three ropes from the balloon to the basket. Using Yellow backstitch the sun's rays. Sew two buttons on shoulder if desired.

Number of Knitting Worsted 2oz balls per size					
Shade	Size in inches				
	22	24	26	28	30
A Yellow	2	2	2	3	3
B Electric blue	1	1	1	2	2
C Chalky blue	2	2	2	3	3
D Dark chocolate	1	1	1	1	1
E Warm brown	1	1	1	1	1
F White	1	1	1	1	1
G Parchment	small quantity				
H Bright pink	small quantity				
I Red	small quantity				
J Royal blue	small quantity				
K Cerise	small quantity				
L Black	scrap				

Barely Afloat

On the sand, just in front of Jed was a bright red boat with yellow sails. He pulled it to the sea, jumped in and started out. It felt great, going up and down, up and down over the waves. He looked back over his shoulder and realized that the shore was quite a long way back. The waves were getting big and a fish leapt out of the water in front of him.

Jed imagined himself falling overboard and being swallowed by this fish. A shiver went down his spine. He turned the boat towards the shore and headed back. "Bears belong back on the beach" he told himself.

◆ BEAR ESSENTIALS ◆

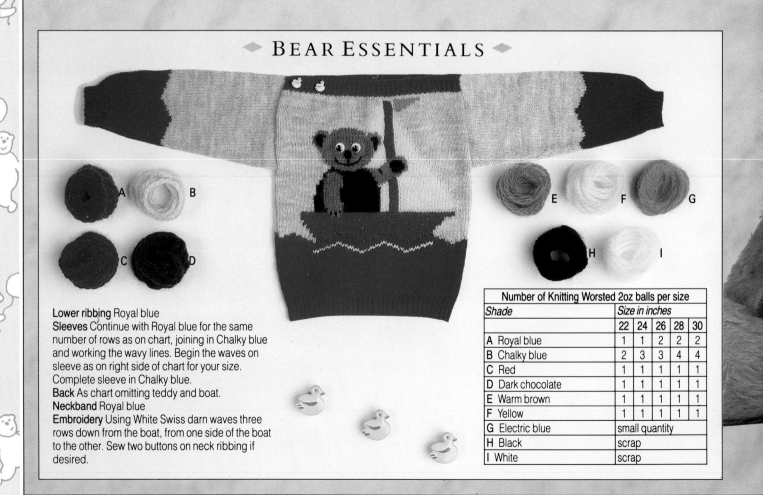

Lower ribbing Royal blue
Sleeves Continue with Royal blue for the same number of rows as on chart, joining in Chalky blue and working the wavy lines. Begin the waves on sleeve as on right side of chart for your size. Complete sleeve in Chalky blue.
Back As chart omitting teddy and boat.
Neckband Royal blue
Embroidery Using White Swiss darn waves three rows down from the boat, from one side of the boat to the other. Sew two buttons on neck ribbing if desired.

Number of Knitting Worsted 2oz balls per size					
Shade	Size in inches				
	22	24	26	28	30
A Royal blue	1	1	2	2	2
B Chalky blue	2	3	3	4	4
C Red	1	1	1	1	1
D Dark chocolate	1	1	1	1	1
E Warm brown	1	1	1	1	1
F Yellow	1	1	1	1	1
G Electric blue	small quantity				
H Black	scrap				
I White	scrap				

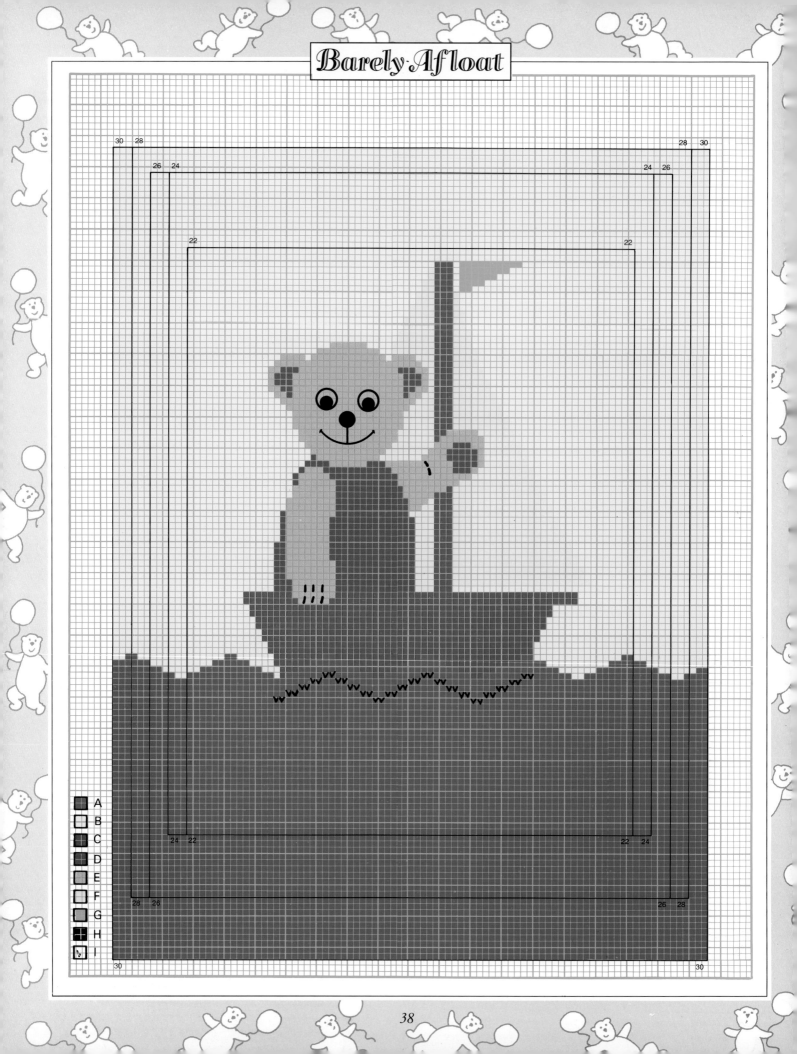

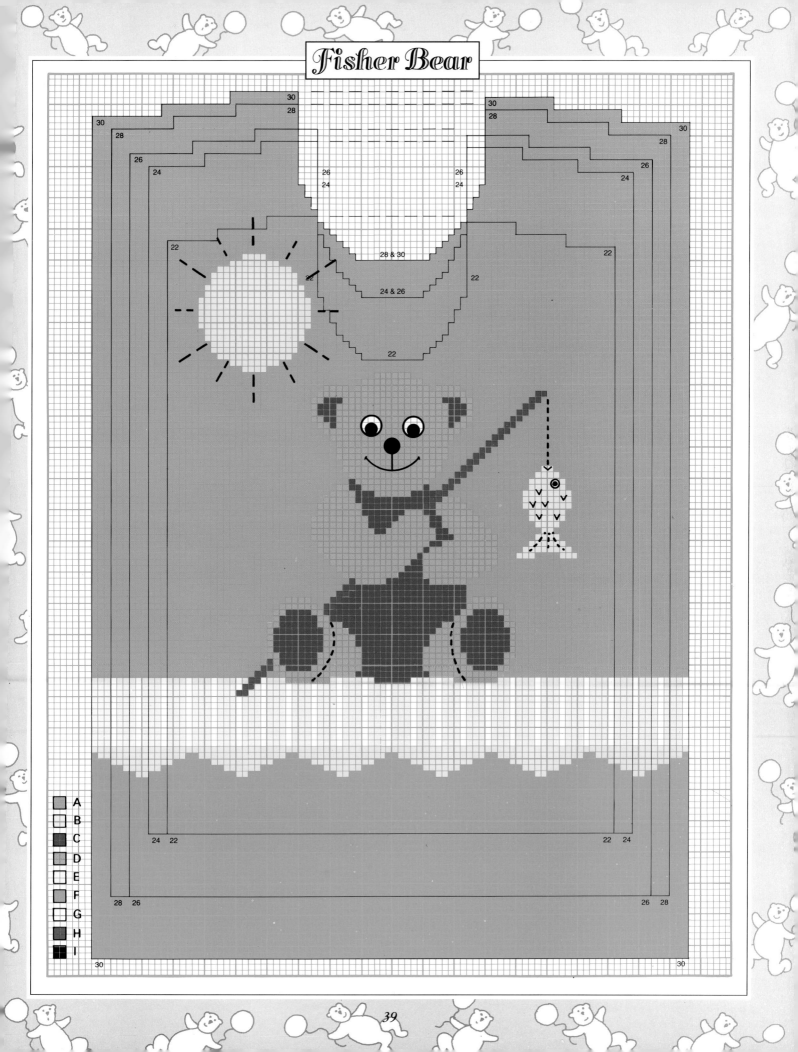

Jed made a rod from a long thin piece of wood, tied some string to the end and added an old hook that he'd found at the bottom of the boat. He sat down on the end of the pier and threw his line into the water. Soon he felt a great tug on the end of his line and out jumped a big yellow fish! "I've caught one," he shouted to nobody in particular.

The fish wiggled on the end of the line "Let me go" he seemed to be saying. Jed threw him back. "I came out to find the rainbow," he thought, "not make another creature unhappy. It's about time I continued my search." And off he went.

◆ BEAR ESSENTIALS ◆

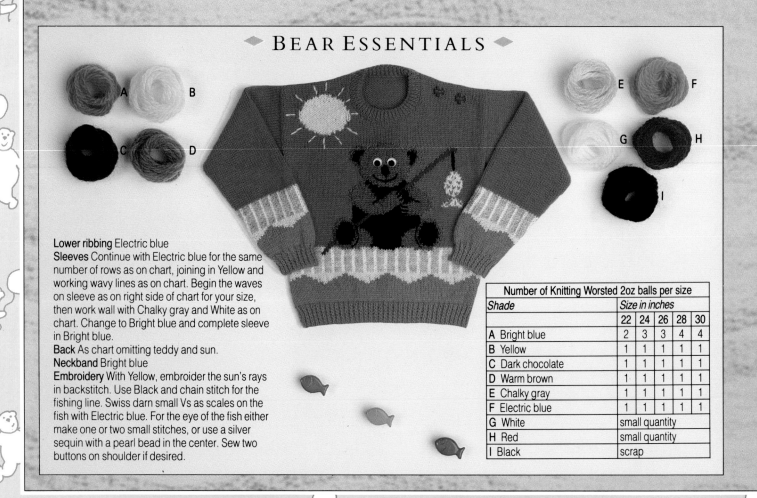

Lower ribbing Electric blue
Sleeves Continue with Electric blue for the same number of rows as on chart, joining in Yellow and working wavy lines as on chart. Begin the waves on sleeve as on right side of chart for your size, then work wall with Chalky gray and White as on chart. Change to Bright blue and complete sleeve in Bright blue.
Back As chart omitting teddy and sun.
Neckband Bright blue
Embroidery With Yellow, embroider the sun's rays in backstitch. Use Black and chain stitch for the fishing line. Swiss darn small Vs as scales on the fish with Electric blue. For the eye of the fish either make one or two small stitches, or use a silver sequin with a pearl bead in the center. Sew two buttons on shoulder if desired.

Number of Knitting Worsted 2oz balls per size					
Shade	Size in inches				
	22	24	26	28	30
A Bright blue	2	3	3	4	4
B Yellow	1	1	1	1	1
C Dark chocolate	1	1	1	1	1
D Warm brown	1	1	1	1	1
E Chalky gray	1	1	1	1	1
F Electric blue	1	1	1	1	1
G White	small quantity				
H Red	small quantity				
I Black	scrap				

Bears in a Basket

Down with a bang came the hot air balloon and Jed saw the most beautiful bear he had ever seen. He immediately fell in love with her. His knees began to wobble. He just had to stop and talk. He climbed into the basket and told her about himself, where he came from, and all his adventures in search of the rainbow.

"Ah the rainbow . . ." the beautiful bear began. But just as she started to tell Jed something very important, a gust of wind rocked the balloon and Jed knocked against a switch and fell out as the balloon suddenly rose in the air. "Goodbye," he shouted to the beautiful bear. "I don't even know your name."

◆ BEAR ESSENTIALS ◆

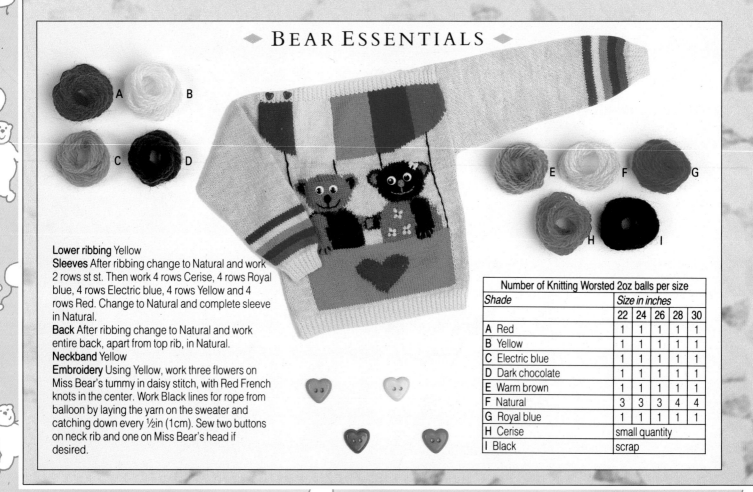

Lower ribbing Yellow
Sleeves After ribbing change to Natural and work 2 rows st st. Then work 4 rows Cerise, 4 rows Royal blue, 4 rows Electric blue, 4 rows Yellow and 4 rows Red. Change to Natural and complete sleeve in Natural.
Back After ribbing change to Natural and work entire back, apart from top rib, in Natural.
Neckband Yellow
Embroidery Using Yellow, work three flowers on Miss Bear's tummy in daisy stitch, with Red French knots in the center. Work Black lines for rope from balloon by laying the yarn on the sweater and catching down every ½in (1cm). Sew two buttons on neck rib and one on Miss Bear's head if desired.

Number of Knitting Worsted 2oz balls per size					
Shade	Size in inches				
	22	24	26	28	30
A Red	1	1	1	1	1
B Yellow	1	1	1	1	1
C Electric blue	1	1	1	1	1
D Dark chocolate	1	1	1	1	1
E Warm brown	1	1	1	1	1
F Natural	3	3	3	4	4
G Royal blue	1	1	1	1	1
H Cerise	small quantity				
I Black	scrap				

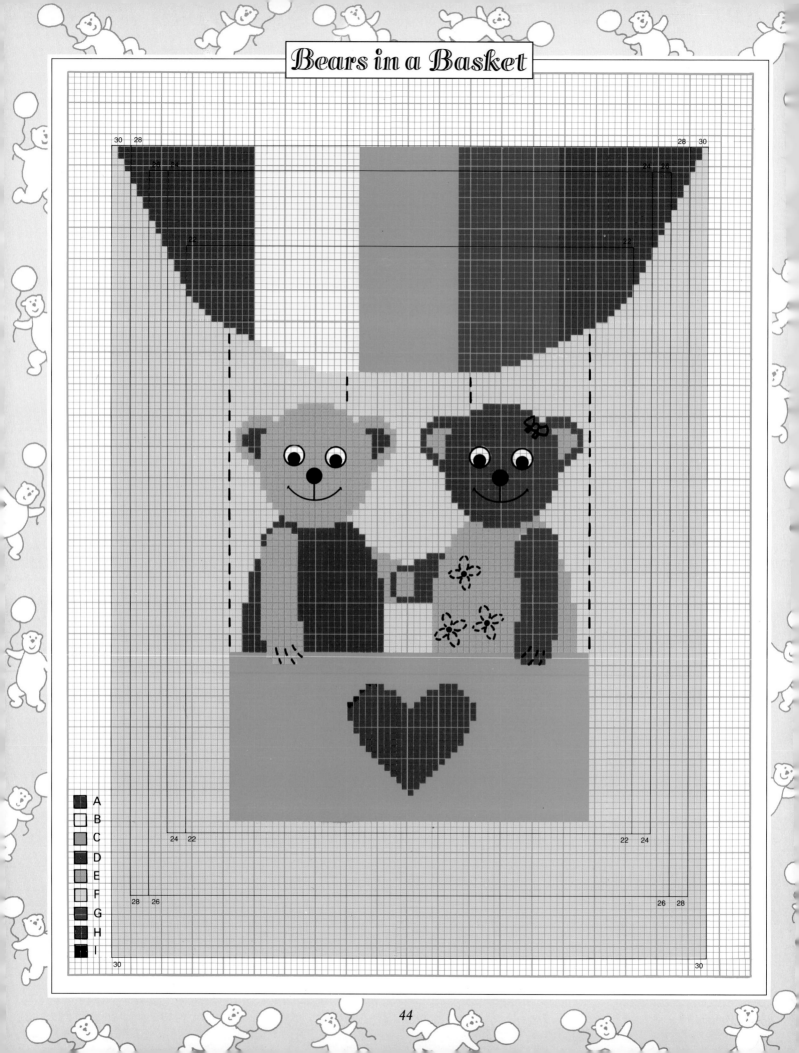

Bears in a Basket

A
B
C
D
E
F
G
H
I

44

Beareft

45

Beareft

Overcome by the beauty of Miss Bear and his misfortune at losing her, Jed set off home. He had gone only a little way when he saw a playground. He sat on a swing and swung backwards and forwards, feeling sorry for himself. Suddenly he heard someone say his name. Next to him was another bear. "I've been watching you on your journey," said the bear. "And I want to help you find the rainbow. I've seen it and touched it. It felt so good that I want you to find it too. The rainbow has changed my life and it can change yours also. To find the rainbow, you must go where the river falls over the rocks."

◆ BEAR ESSENTIALS ◆

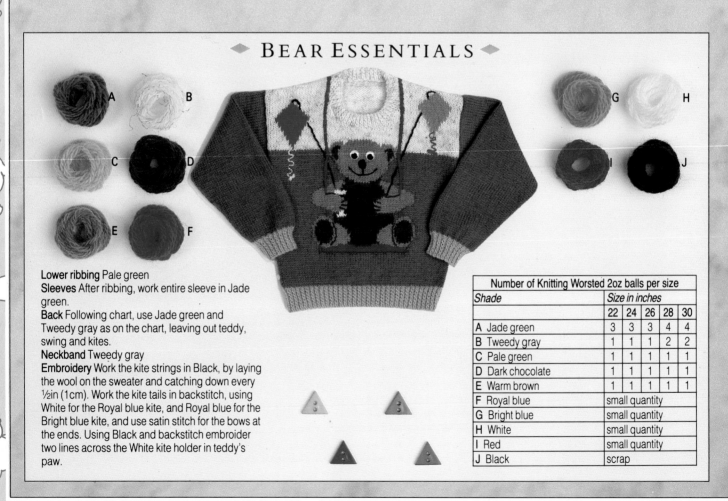

Lower ribbing Pale green
Sleeves After ribbing, work entire sleeve in Jade green.
Back Following chart, use Jade green and Tweedy gray as on the chart, leaving out teddy, swing and kites.
Neckband Tweedy gray
Embroidery Work the kite strings in Black, by laying the wool on the sweater and catching down every ½in (1cm). Work the kite tails in backstitch, using White for the Royal blue kite, and Royal blue for the Bright blue kite, and use satin stitch for the bows at the ends. Using Black and backstitch embroider two lines across the White kite holder in teddy's paw.

Number of Knitting Worsted 2oz balls per size					
Shade	Size in inches				
	22	24	26	28	30
A Jade green	3	3	3	4	4
B Tweedy gray	1	1	1	2	2
C Pale green	1	1	1	1	1
D Dark chocolate	1	1	1	1	1
E Warm brown	1	1	1	1	1
F Royal blue	small quantity				
G Bright blue	small quantity				
H White	small quantity				
I Red	small quantity				
J Black	scrap				

Rainbow Bear

Without knowing quite how he'd arrived there, Jed found himself at a waterfall close to the most beautiful rainbow he had ever seen. He waded into the water to the top of the waterfall and saw the rainbow right in front of him. He walked out and began to slide down the waterfall, first his feet, then his legs, tummy, arms and head — all went through the rainbow. As Jed passed through the different colors he felt a glow grow inside him. He was bubbling over with happiness. He had found the rainbow, touched the rainbow and now felt happier than he had ever dreamed he would.

◆ BEAR ESSENTIALS

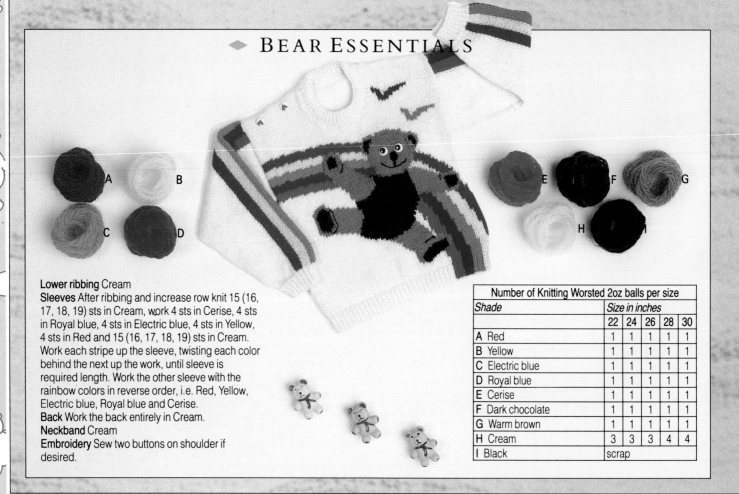

Lower ribbing Cream
Sleeves After ribbing and increase row knit 15 (16, 17, 18, 19) sts in Cream, work 4 sts in Cerise, 4 sts in Royal blue, 4 sts in Electric blue, 4 sts in Yellow, 4 sts in Red and 15 (16, 17, 18, 19) sts in Cream. Work each stripe up the sleeve, twisting each color behind the next up the work, until sleeve is required length. Work the other sleeve with the rainbow colors in reverse order, i.e. Red, Yellow, Electric blue, Royal blue and Cerise.
Back Work the back entirely in Cream.
Neckband Cream
Embroidery Sew two buttons on shoulder if desired.

Number of Knitting Worsted 2oz balls per size					
Shade	Size in inches				
	22	24	26	28	30
A Red	1	1	1	1	1
B Yellow	1	1	1	1	1
C Electric blue	1	1	1	1	1
D Royal blue	1	1	1	1	1
E Cerise	1	1	1	1	1
F Dark chocolate	1	1	1	1	1
G Warm brown	1	1	1	1	1
H Cream	3	3	3	4	4
I Black	scrap				

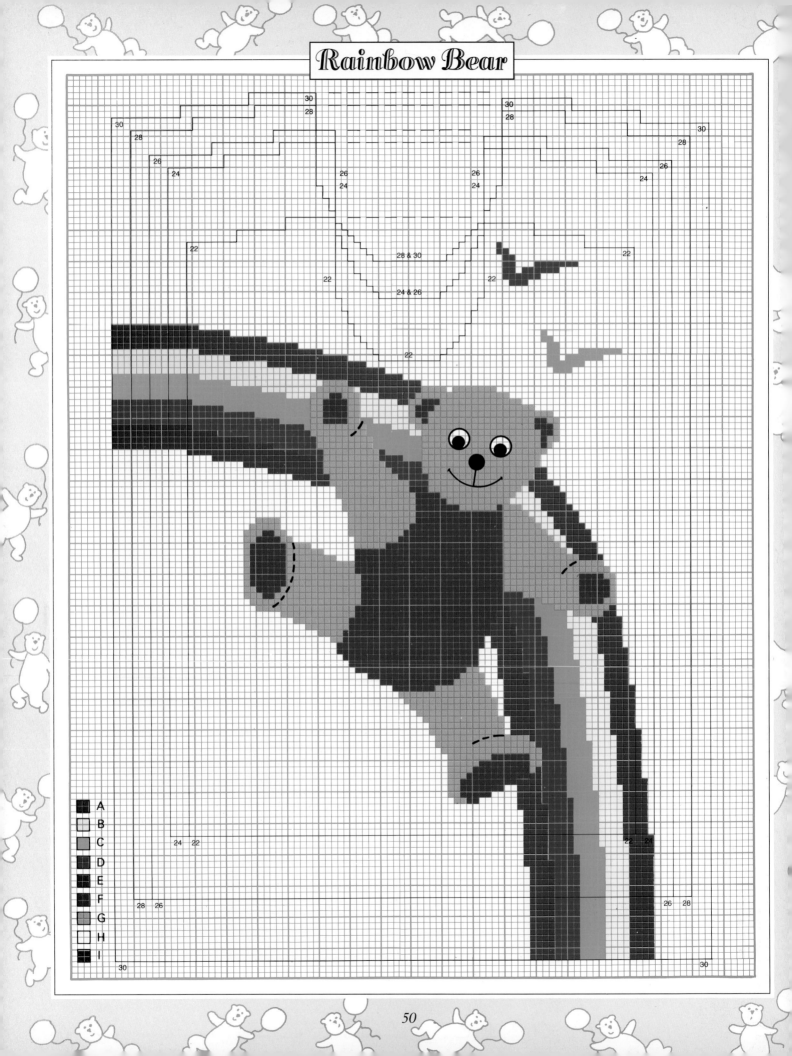

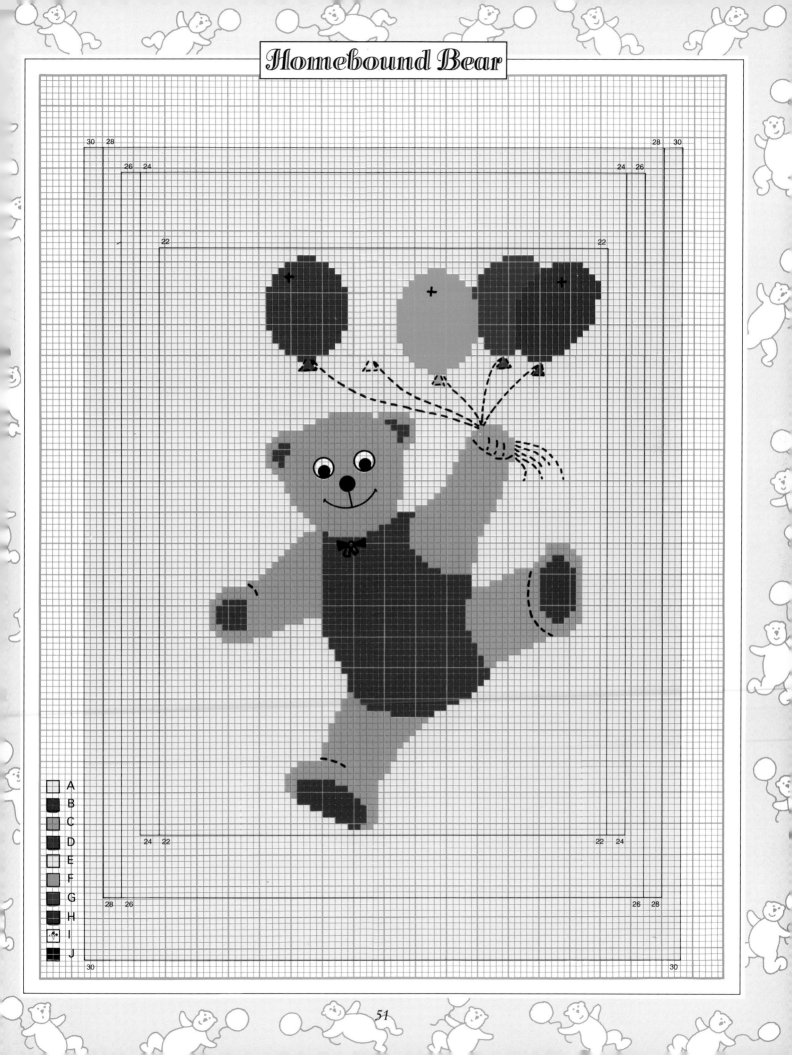

Homebound Bear

Homebound Bear

Jed felt so happy he did a little dance. Underneath the rainbow he began to hop, skip and jump, raising his hands towards the sky. Although he could no longer touch the rainbow, he felt its happiness inside him and knew he would always feel it.

Now he was ready to go home.

But how could he get back when he was so far away? Suddenly he had an idea. He took out the balloons that all bears kept for emergencies. Surely they would carry home such a light-hearted happy bear as he was, a bear who was bringing the rainbow's message to all who needed it everywhere.

◆ BEAR ESSENTIALS ◆

Lower ribbing Work in stripes as follows: Cast on with Red and work 2 rows rib, change to Yellow and knit 1 row, work 2 rows rib, change to Electric blue and purl 1 row, work 2 rows rib, change to Royal blue and knit 1 row, work 2 rows rib, change to Cerise and purl 1 row, work 2 rows rib.

Sleeves After striped ribbing change to Tweedy gray and complete sleeve in Tweedy gray.

Back After striped ribbing change to Tweedy gray and work entire back in Tweedy gray.

Neckband Red

Embroidery Using Black, work the strings of the balloons in chain stitch. Using two stitches of White work a white cross on the Red, Electric blue and Cerise balloons. Using the different colors of the respective balloons, outline and fill in a small triangle at the bottom of each balloon. Sew two buttons on neck rib if desired.

Number of Knitting Worsted 2oz balls per size					
Shade	Size in inches				
	22	24	26	28	30
A Tweedy gray	4	4	4	5	5
B Dark chocolate	1	1	1	1	1
C Warm brown	1	1	1	1	1
D Red	1	1	1	1	1
E Yellow	1	1	1	1	1
F Electric blue	1	1	1	1	1
G Royal blue	1	1	1	1	1
H Cerise	1	1	1	1	1
I White	scrap				
J Black	scrap				

Basic Ted-niques

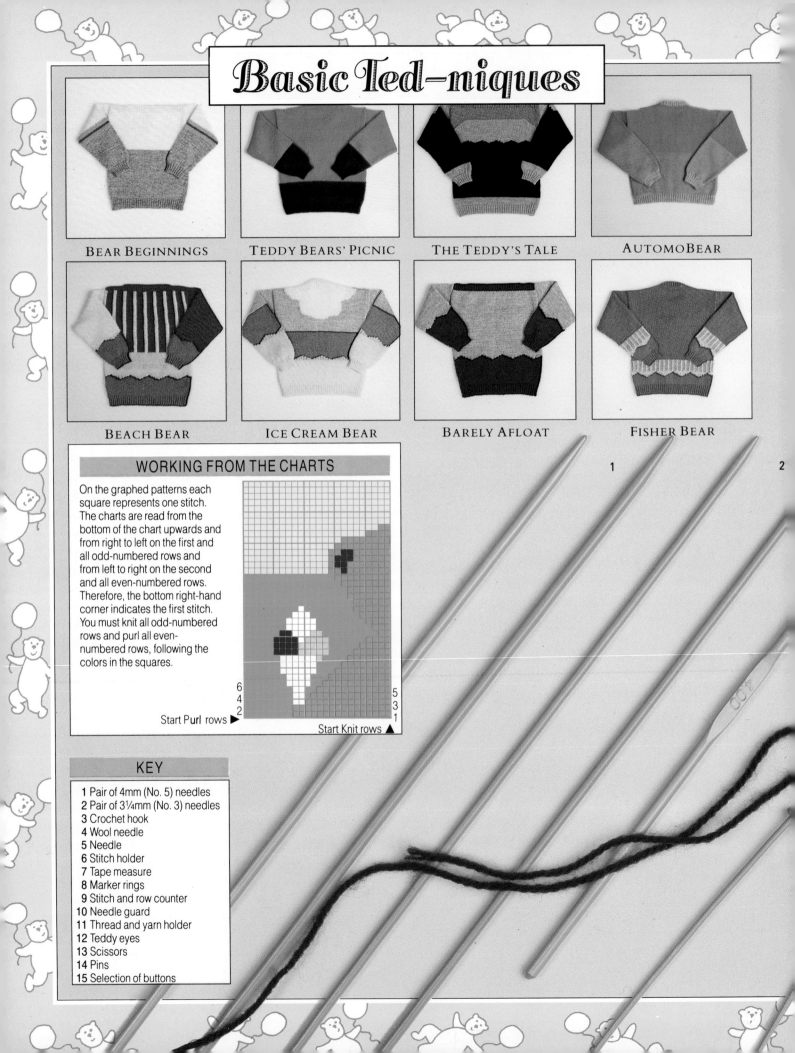

BEAR BEGINNINGS   TEDDY BEARS' PICNIC   THE TEDDY'S TALE   AUTOMOBEAR

BEACH BEAR   ICE CREAM BEAR   BARELY AFLOAT   FISHER BEAR

WORKING FROM THE CHARTS

On the graphed patterns each square represents one stitch. The charts are read from the bottom of the chart upwards and from right to left on the first and all odd-numbered rows and from left to right on the second and all even-numbered rows. Therefore, the bottom right-hand corner indicates the first stitch. You must knit all odd-numbered rows and purl all even-numbered rows, following the colors in the squares.

6
4
2
Start Purl rows ▶

5
3
1
Start Knit rows ▲

1

2

KEY

1 Pair of 4mm (No. 5) needles
2 Pair of 3¼mm (No. 3) needles
3 Crochet hook
4 Wool needle
5 Needle
6 Stitch holder
7 Tape measure
8 Marker rings
9 Stitch and row counter
10 Needle guard
11 Thread and yarn holder
12 Teddy eyes
13 Scissors
14 Pins
15 Selection of buttons

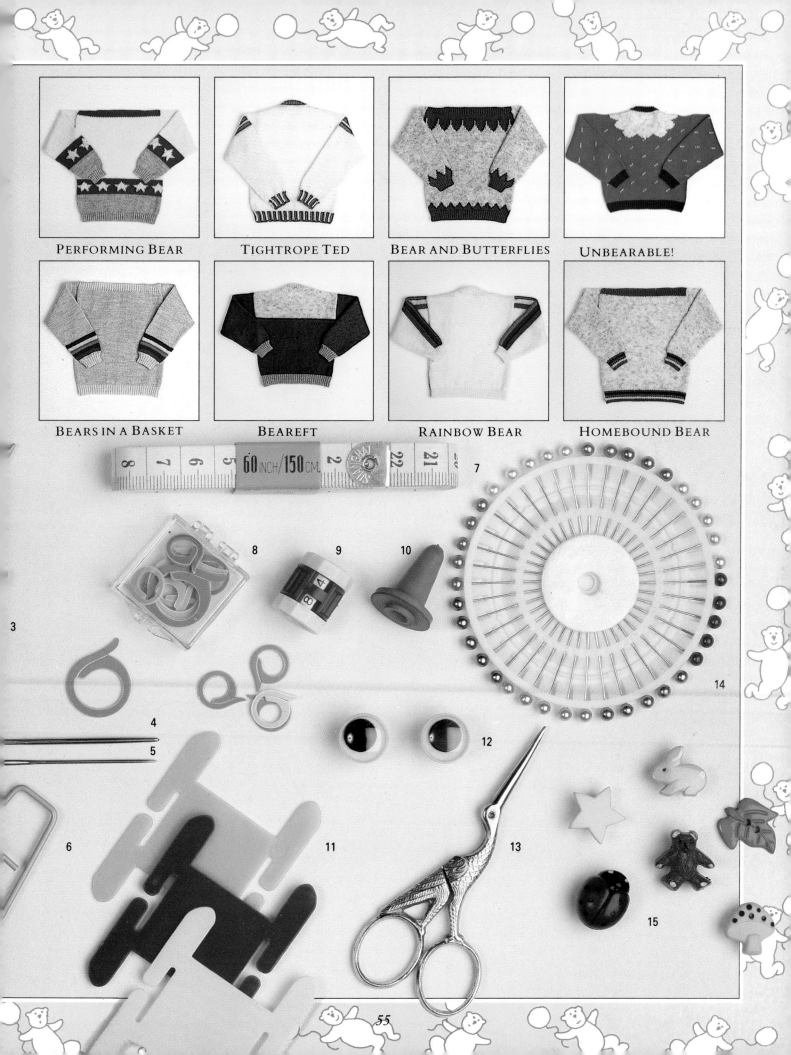

PERFORMING BEAR

TIGHTROPE TED

BEAR AND BUTTERFLIES

UNBEARABLE!

BEARS IN A BASKET

BEAREFT

RAINBOW BEAR

HOMEBOUND BEAR

7

3

8

9

10

14

4

5

12

6

11

13

15

55

Beginning to Knit

When you begin to work on a pattern placing the first row of stitches on the needle is known as 'casting on'. All further rows are worked into these initial loops. This can be done on one or two needles and the method may be specified in the pattern.

SINGLE CAST ON

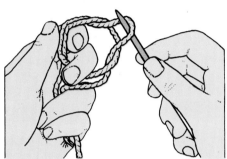

1 Wrap your yarn around two fingers twice and pull a loop through the twisted yarn with a knitting needle.

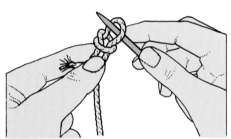

2 Pull both ends of the yarn to tighten. This produces a slip loop.

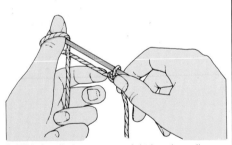

3 With the slip loop on your right-hand needle wrap the working end of the yarn around your left thumb and hold it in the palm of your hand. Put the needle through the yarn behind the thumb.

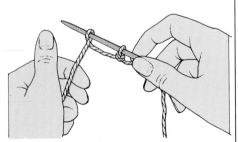

4 Lift the yarn and slide the new 'stitch' towards the slip loop. Tighten the working end to secure the stitch until you have the required number.

TWO-NEEDLE CAST ON

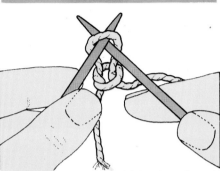

1 With the slip loop on your left-hand needle, insert your right-hand needle through the loop from front to back.

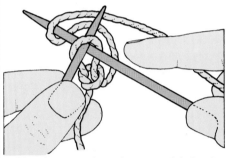

2 Bring the yarn under and over your right-hand needle.

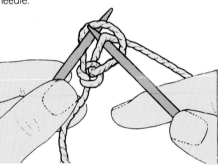

3 Draw up the yarn through the slip loop to make a stitch.

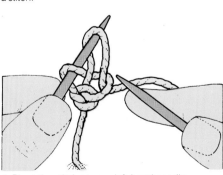

4 Place the stitch on your left-hand needle. Continue to make stitches drawing the yarn through the last stitch on your left-hand needle.

BINDING OFF

When you end a piece of knitting you must secure all the stitches you have finished by "binding off". This should be done on a knit row but you can employ the same technique on a purl row: the stitches, whether knit or purl, should be made loosely. When binding off rib, you must use both knit and purl.

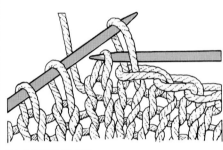

IN A KNIT ROW

1 Knit the first two stitches and insert the tip of your left-hand needle through the first stitch.

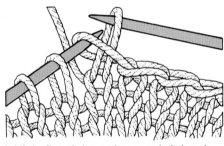

2 Lift the first stitch over the second stitch and discard it. Knit the next stitch and continue to lift the first stitch over the second stitch to the end of the row. Be careful not to knit too tightly. For the last stitch, cut your yarn, slip the end through the stitch and pull the yarn tight to fasten off securely.

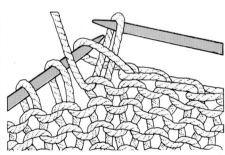

IN A PURL ROW

Purl the first two (and all subsequent) stitches and continue as for knit stitch above.

Basic Stitches

Knit stitch and purl stitch are the two basic knitting stitches. Either one worked continuously in rows forms Garter stitch pattern and worked alternately forms Stockinette stitch pattern.

KNIT STITCH (K)

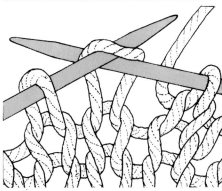

1 With the yarn at the back, insert your right-hand needle from front to back into the first stitch on your left-hand needle.

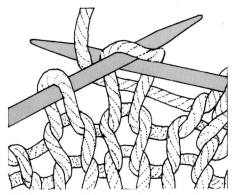

2 Bring your working yarn under and over the point of your right-hand needle.

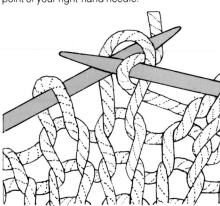

3 Draw a loop through and slide the first stitch off your left-hand needle while the new stitch is retained on your right-hand needle. Continue in this way to the end of the row.

4 To knit the next row, turn the work around so that the back is facing you and the worked stitches are held on the needle in your left hand. Proceed to make stitches as above, with the initially empty needle held in your right hand.

PURL STITCH (P)

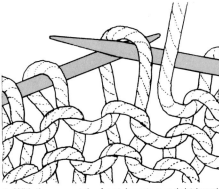

1 With the yarn at the front, insert your right-hand needle from back to front into the first stitch on your left-hand needle.

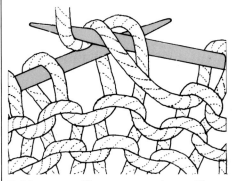

2 Bring your working yarn over and around the point of your right-hand needle.

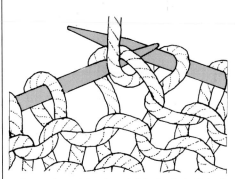

3 Draw a loop through and slide the first stitch off your right-hand needle while the new stitch is retained on your right-hand needle. Continue in this way to the end of the row.

4 To purl the next row, turn the work around so that the back is facing you and the worked stitches are held on the needle in your left hand. Proceed to makes stitches as above, with the initially empty needle held in your right hand.

STOCKINETTE STITCH (st st)

Knitting the first and every odd row and purling the second and every even row produces Stockinette stitch when made on two needles.

RIBBING

A combination of knit and purl stitches, usually one or two knit stitches and then one or two purl stitches, in the same row is known as ribbing. Ribbing is used on sleeve and body edges to form a neat, stretchable finish. It is usually worked on smaller needles than the main body of the garment.

STITCH GAUGE

Before starting to make any garment you must make a tension sample in order to measure stitch gauge. You should do this in order to check your individual control of the yarn against the pattern you are following, so that the desired measurements are the same as in the pattern.

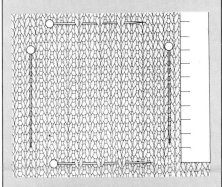

The stitch gauge, or tension, is always given at the beginning of a pattern. It is written as the number of stitches, and the number of rows in a particular pattern, e.g. stockinette stitch, to a specified size, such as 4in (10cm), using the yarn and needles called for in the pattern. An example is 32 sts and 32 rows to 4in (10cm) over st st pattern on No.5 (4mm) needles.

A variation in tension within a garment will result in an uneven appearance. By knitting the required number of stitches and rows, your sample will reveal whether the yarn and needles you are using will make up into the size and shape you require. When working your tension sample, you must take into account the pattern and the method of carrying yarns across the back of the work (see p. 59).

Correcting Mistakes

DROPPED STITCHES

Occasionally, a stitch may fall off your needle, in which case correct it by following one of the techniques described below. Dropped stitches are often the result of leaving work in the middle of a row.

LADDERS

If a dropped stitch is left, it can unravel down the work and form a "ladder". The easiest way to correct this is to use a crochet hook to pick up the stitches in pattern, although you can try to correct it with your needles.

If you make a mistake in your knitting, you may have to "unpick" a stitch, which can result in a ladder. Pick up one dropped stitch at a time, securing any others with a safety pin to prevent further unravelling.

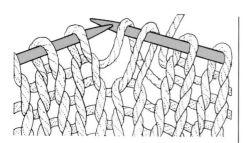

PICKING UP A DROPPED KNIT STITCH

1 Pick up both the stitch and strand on your right-hand needle, inserting the needle from front to back.

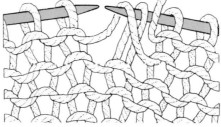

PICKING UP A DROPPED PURL STITCH

1 Pick up both the stitch and strand on your right-hand needle, inserting the needle from back to front.

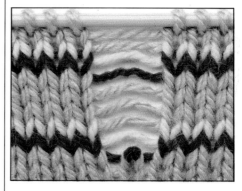

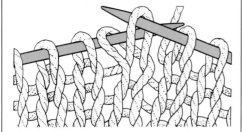

2 Insert your left-hand needle through the stitch only, from back to front. With your right-hand needle only, pull the strand through the stitch to make the extra stitch. (Drop the stitch from your left-hand needle.)

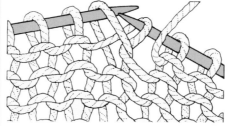

2 Insert your left-hand needle through the stitch only, from front to back. With your right-hand needle only, pull the strand through the stitch to make the extra stitch. (Drop the stitch from your left-hand needle.)

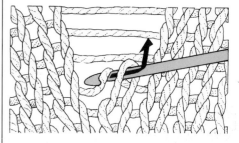

CORRECTING A KNIT LADDER

Insert a crochet hook through the front of the dropped stitch. Hook up one strand and pull it through the stitch to form a new stitch one row up. Continue in this way to the top of the ladder then continue in pattern.

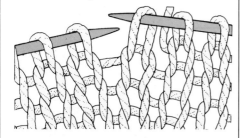

3 Transfer the re-formed stitch back to your left-hand needle, so that it untwists and faces the correct way. It is now ready for knitting again.

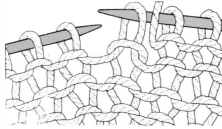

3 Transfer the re-formed stitch back to your left-hand needle, so that it untwists and faces the correct way. It is now ready for purling again.

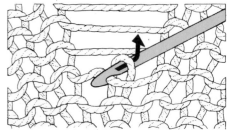

CORRECTING A PURL LADDER

Insert a crochet hook through the back of the dropped stitch. Hook up one strand and pull it through the stitch to form a new stitch one row up. Continue to re-insert hook to make stitches until you reach the top of the ladder, then continue in pattern.

UNPICKING MISTAKES

Holding the stitch on your right-hand needle insert your left-hand needle into the row below and undo the stitch. Transfer the stitch back to your right-hand needle and repeat undoing until the error has been reached. Correct stitch as for a ladder, see right.

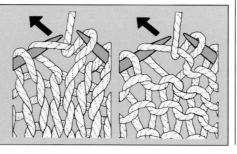

Working with Colors

When knitting with more than one color, you will find it necessary to adopt various techniques to keep the back of the work neat and to prevent holes appearing. There are three basic methods of working: stranding, weaving and crossing. Stranding and weaving produce a thicker fabric.

ADDING YARN AT THE BEGINNING OF A ROW

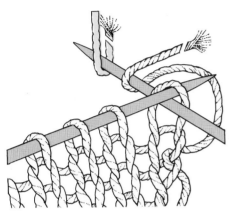

1 Insert your right-hand needle through the first stitch on your left-hand needle and wrap the old yarn, and then the new yarn over it. Knit (or purl) the stitch using both yarns.

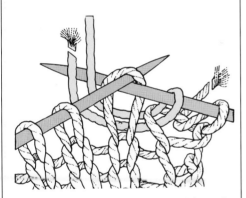

2 Leaving the old yarn at the back, knit (or purl) the next two stitches using the double length of the new yarn.

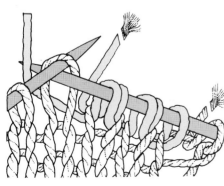

3 Discard the short end of the new yarn and continue to knit as usual. On the following row, treat the three double stitches as single stitches.

ADDING A YARN IN THE MIDDLE OF A ROW

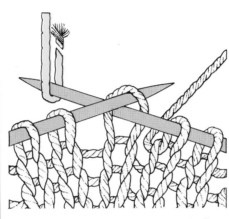

1 Insert your right-hand needle through the first stitch on your left-hand needle. Wrap the new yarn over, and knit (or purl) the stitch with the new yarn. Leave the old yarn at the back of the work.

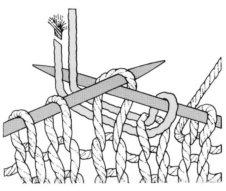

2 Knit (or purl) the next two stitches using the double length of the new yarn.

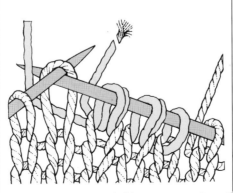

3 Discard the short end of the new yarn and continue to knit as usual. On the following row, treat the two double stitches as single stitches.

STRANDING YARN

Use this method for working narrow stripes, and other patterns requiring only two colors in a row. Strand yarn over a maximum of five stitches only.

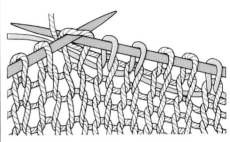

IN A KNIT ROW

With both yarns at the back of the work, knit the required number of stitches with yarn A (in this case two), and then drop it to the back. Pick up yarn B and knit the required number of stitches and then drop it to the back. Both yarns should be stranded loosely along the back of the work.

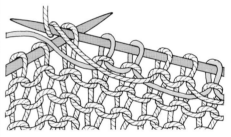

IN A PURL ROW

With both yarns at the front of the work, purl the required number of stitches with yarn A (in this case two), and then drop it. Pick up yarn B and purl the required number of stitches and then drop it. Both yarns should be stranded loosely along the front (side facing you).

WINDING BOBBINS

To help keep different yarns separate when working complicated color patterns, wind manageable lengths onto bobbins, yarn holders or spools. Replenish as necessary. Or, keep yarns in individual plastic bags secured at the "neck" with an elastic band.

Working with Colors

WEAVING YARN

This method should be used when you are working large pattern repeats, for patterns requiring three or more colors, and when yarn has to be carried over more than five stitches.

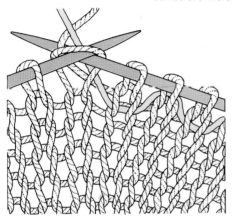

IN A KNIT ROW

1 Hold yarn A in your right hand and yarn B in your left hand to the back of the work.

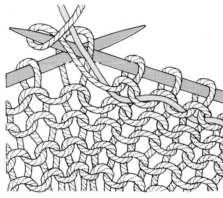

IN A PURL ROW

1 Hold yarn A in your right hand and yarn B in your left hand to the front of the work.

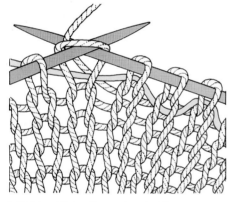

2 Knit one stitch with yarn A and, at the same time, bring yarn B below yarn A. When yarn B is being used, weave yarn A as above.

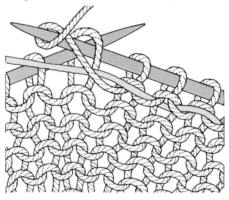

2 Purl one stitch with yarn A but this time bring yarn B below yarn A. When yarn B is being used, weave yarn A as above.

CROSSING COLORS

Use this method for working solid blocks of color. When crossing colors each color is kept as a separate ball or on a bobbin and is not taken across the work. Rather, the yarns are crossed at the join. Follow the instructions below for vertical colour patterns as well, but cross the colors on every row.

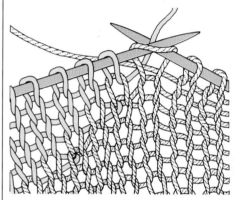

IN A KNIT ROW FOR A DIAGONAL STRIPE TO THE RIGHT

Cross yarn A in front of yarn B and drop it to the back. Knit the first stitch on your left-hand needle using yarn B. On the return row the yarns will automatically loop together.

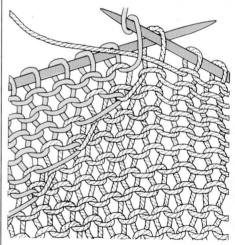

IN A PURL ROW FOR A DIAGONAL STRIPE TO THE LEFT

Pick up yarn B in front of yarn A and use it to purl the next stitch on your left-hand needle. On the return row, the yarns will automatically loop together.

CHECKING YOUR TECHNIQUE

WEAVING

If you have worked weaving correctly, the yarns will cross evenly and remain at the same depth. A "smocking" effect means that you have pulled the yarns too tightly. It is better for the yarns to be woven too loosely than too tightly.

STRANDING

If you have worked stranding correctly, the yarns will be running evenly across the back of the work at the same tension as the knitting.

Puckering indicates that you have pulled the yarns too tightly.

Other Techniques

SEAMS

Your pattern will usually set out the order of seaming: normally the shoulder seams are joined first if you have to pick up stitches to make the neck band. There is a choice of two methods, the edge-to-edge seam and the backstitch seam.

An edge-to-edge seam is useful on lightweight knits because it is almost invisible and forms no ridge.

A backstitch seam is stronger and firmer and is suitable for all garments but it forms a ridge.

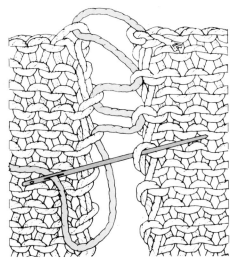

EDGE-TO-EDGE SEAM

Place the pieces to be joined edge-to-edge with the "heads" of the knit stitches locking together. Match the pattern pieces carefully row for row and stitch for stitch. Using the main yarn, sew into the head of each stitch alternately.

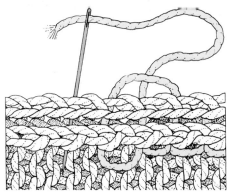

BACKSTITCH SEAM

Place the pieces to be joined together with their right sides facing. Carefully match pattern to pattern, row to row and stitch to stitch. Sew along the seam using backstitch sewing into the center of each stitch to correspond with the stitch on the opposite piece. Sew ¼in (6mm) in from the edge of the knitting.

INCREASING

INCREASE 1 (Inc 1)

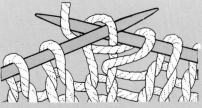

IN A KNIT ROW

Knit into the front of the stitch in the usual way. Without discarding the stitch on your left-hand needle, knit into the back of it, making two stitches.

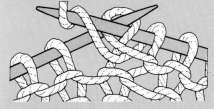

IN A PURL ROW

Purl into the front of the stitch in the usual way. Without discarding the stitch on your left-hand needle, purl into the back of it, making two stitches.

DECREASING

KNITTING TWO STITCHES TOGETHER (K2 tog)

IN A KNIT ROW (K2 tog)

Insert your right-hand needle through the front of the first two stitches on your left-hand needle. Knit them together as a single stitch.

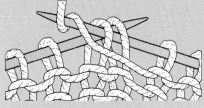

IN A PURL ROW (P2 tog)

Insert your right-hand needle through the front of the first two stitches on your left-hand needle. Purl them together as a single stitch.

FINISHING TECHNIQUES

Before pattern pieces are joined up, they are usually blocked and pressed to ensure a good fit. It's always a good idea to check the yarn band for any special instructions. The pieces are blocked when dry and are pressed with a cloth.

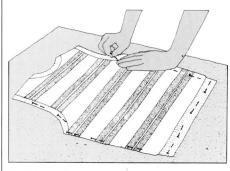

BLOCKING

Garment pieces need blocking, or putting into shape before they can be joined up. Cover a table with a folded blanket and a sheet. Using rustless pins, "block" the pieces wrong-side out to the correct measurements. Be careful not to stretch or distort the fabric and make sure that all the rows run in straight lines.

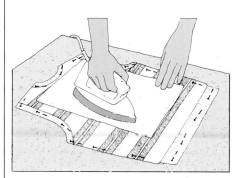

PRESSING

After blocking, the garment pieces are usually pressed in position. Use a warm iron and a cloth on wool. Lay the iron on the fabric and lift it up, do not move it over the surface. Do not remove any of the pins until the work has cooled and dried completely.

Ribbing should be lightly stretched and pinned before ironing. Use a heavy cloth and remove the pins in order to adjust the fabric while it is still warm.

Embroidery

SWISS DARNING

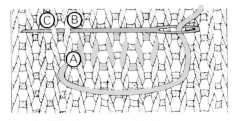

WORKING HORIZONTALLY

1 Secure the embroidery yarn at the back of the work and bring your needle out to the front of the work at A. Insert the needle at B, under the base of the stitch above, and bring it out at C.

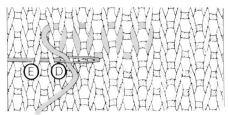

2 Insert the needle at D and emerge at E ready to embroider the next stitch.

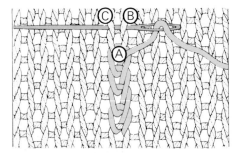

WORKING VERTICALLY

1 Secure the embroidery yarn at the back of the work and bring your needle out to the front of the work at A. Insert the needle at B, bringing it out at C.

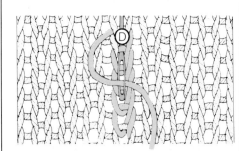

2 Take the needle under the head of the stitch below and emerge above it at D, ready to form the next stitch.

SATIN STITCH

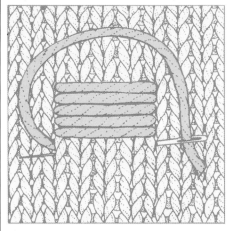

For best results, work horizontal straight stitches. The stitches should fit closely together, giving a very smooth surface and straight outside edges.

FRENCH KNOT

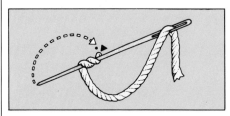

Holding thread down with left thumb, encircle thread twice with needle. Then twist needle back to arrow and insert it close to starting point. Pull through to back before repositioning for next stitch.

ADDING BEADS AND SEQUINS

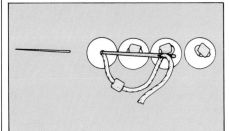

Bring the needle out through the eye of the sequin and thread on a small bead, then insert the needle back through the eye of the sequin and pull tight so that the bead rests firmly over the eye, securing the sequin.

CHAIN STITCH

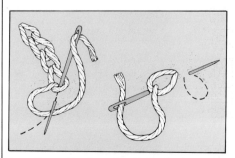

Loop the working thread under the tip of your needle and hold it down with your left thumb while you pick up some of the ground fabric in each stitch. The needle is inserted into the same hole from which it has emerged.

To make a leaf shape, bring out your needle and insert it into the same spot bringing it out with a loop under the needle. Take it over the loop so that you make a small tying stitch to anchor it.

BACKSTITCH

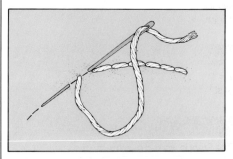

Work in small, even stitches by first making a stitch forwards and then a stitch backwards.

STEM STITCH

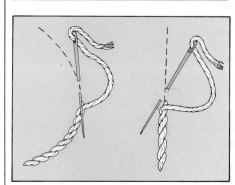

Work the stitch with the thread kept on the same side of the needle. For a wider effect, insert the needle into the ground fabric at a slight angle. The greater the angle, the wider the effect.

Bear Wear

MEASUREMENTS

To fit chest	22 (24,26,28,30)in
	56 (61,66,71,76)cm
Actual chest measurement	24 (26,28,30,32)in
of garment	61 (66,71,76,81)cm
Sleeve length	12 (14,15,16,17)in
(finished)	31 (36,38,41,43)cm

MATERIALS

Knitting Worsted as found with each adventure in **Bear Essentials.**
1 pair of 3¼mm (No.3) needles
1 pair of 4mm (No.5) needles
2 buttons (optional)
2 15mm safety goo-goo eyes (or embroidery thread)

TENSION

12 sts and 15 rows measure 2in (5cm) over stockinette stitch on No.5 (4mm) needles (or size needed to obtain this tension)

ABBREVIATIONS

k = knit; p = purl; k1b = knit into back of stitch; st st = stockinette stitch; st(s) = stitch(es)

WORKING NOTES

The **Front** is worked by following the appropriate chart (see **Working from charts,** p.54). All odd-number rows are knit rows worked from right to left, all even-number rows are purl rows worked from left to right, forming stocking stitch. The Back is worked by following the chart for the main background colors only, leaving out the motifs (see **Bear Essentials,** and photographs of sweater backs, pp.54–5).

The yarn for large blocks of color should be carried up the work, not along the back, the yarn for smaller areas of color should be woven in. See working with colors, pp.59 and 60.

FRONT

With No.3 (3¼mm) needles and appropriate color(s) for ribbing (as given under **Bear Essentials** for each pattern), cast on 72 (78,84,90,96) sts and work 12 rows in twisted rib as follows: k1, p1, *k1b, p1, repeat from * to end of row. Change to No.5 (4mm) needles and work stockinette stitch following the chart for color changes. Begin at row 1 for size 30, row 11 for

sizes 26 and 28 and row 21 for sizes 22 and 24.
For the crew neck style, work the neck shaping as indicated by leaving the center 10 (10,10,12,12) sts on a stitch holder. Finish each side separately dec 1 stitch each side of neck edge as indicated on chart. Work to end of chart following shoulder shapings for appropriate sizes.
For the boat neck, omit the neck shaping and work over all sts to start of shoulder shaping, ending with a row on wrong side. Change to No.3 (3¼mm) needles and appropriate color, knit 1 row then work 7 rows twisted rib over all sts. Bind off right across in rib.

BACK

Work rib as for Front in the same color(s). Continue in st st following the chart but leaving out all motifs, working in background colors only, changing from one to another as on the Front of individual pattern (see photograph of sweater backs pp.54–5).
For the crew neck omit front neck shaping. When shoulder shapings are done leave remaining 24 (24,24,30,30) sts across back neck on a stitch holder.
For boat neck finish back exactly as for front.

SLEEVES

With No.3 (3¼mm) needles and appropriate color for sleeve ribbing (see **Bear Essentials**), cast on 37 (39,41,43,45) sts and work 12 rows twisted rib as for Front. On last row of rib increase 13 sts evenly across. Change to No.5 (4mm) needles and work in stockinette stitch, increasing each end of the 5th and every following 6th row until 70 (74,78,82,88) sts, *at the same time* following instructions and color changes of individual pattern. Continue until sleeve measures 12 (14, 15, 16, 17)in, 30 (36,38,41,43)cm, or length required. Bind off loosely with a No.5 (4mm) needle.

NECKBAND

For crew neck only. With rights sides together, sew one shoulder seam. With No.3 (3¼mm) needles, knit 24 (24,24,30,30)sts across Back, pick up 26 (28,28,28,30)sts down side of neck, knit 10 (10,10,12,12)sts from stitch holder, pick up 26 (28,28,28,30) sts up other side of neck: 86 (90,90,98,102)sts. Work 6 (6,6,8,8) rows of twisted rib, knit 1 row, then work 6 (6,6,8,8) more rows of twisted rib. Bind off loosely with a No.5 (4mm) needle.

FINISHING

Block and press (see page 61). Using brown thread and backstitch embroider the bear's body – creases, paws, neck – as indicated on the pattern chart. Either attach two 15mm safety eyes to bear's face, or embroider two eyes in place. Using black wool, work the nose in satin stitch and the mouth in backstitch. Work any further embroidery as given on **Bear Essentials** following charts. Sew on decorative buttons as required.

ATTACHING SAFETY EYES

Push the eye through the knitting, then push the backing firmly in place.

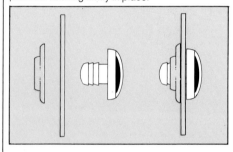

EMBROIDERING EYES

With scrap of white yarn embroider larger circle in satin stitch. Then, using scrap of black yarn, make a smaller circle in satin stitch.

To make back of head With No.5 (4mm) needles and brown yarn, cast on 18 sts and work in st st for 18 rows, cast off. With wrong sides together, sew this to the back of the bear's head to encase the back of the eyes. If you like, add a little stuffing to make the face stand out.
Crew neck version Sew the other shoulder seam. Fold the neckband in half to the wrong side and sew loosely in place.
Boat neck version Oversew shoulder edges together for 1½–2in (3–5cm) from outside edges, leaving central neck opening.
Both versions Sew in sleeves. Darn in all the ends from the motifs and changes of color. With a fine backstitch, sew up side and sleeve seams, oversewing over ribbing. Press again if necessary, avoiding safety eyes.

Washing instructions If you are using safety eyes and buttons, the sweaters should be hand washed and not tumble-dried. Otherwise, they can be washed on a wool setting and left to dry. Press under a dry cloth, avoiding eyes and buttons.

YARN SUPPLIERS

The following manufacturers all bring out a wide range of natural and synthetic yarns.

AUNT LYDIA'S
Talon American
PO Box 3823
Stamford, Connecticut
06905

SUSAN BATES INC.
212 Middlesex Avenue
Chester, Connecticut
06412

BRUNSWICK YARNS
PO Box 276
off Sangamo Road
Pickens, South Carolina
29671

BUCILLA
Sales Service Dept.
150 Meadowlands Pkwy.
Secaucus, New Jersey
07094

CARON INTERNATIONAL
Handknitting yarns and crafts
Box 300
Rochelle, Illinois
61068

CASCADE TEXTILE CORP.
325 East Grand Avenue
South San Francisco, California
94080

COATS & CLARK INC.
Attn: CEAD
72 Cummings Point Road
Stamford, Connecticut
06904

COLUMBIA MINERVA YARNS
Handknitting yarns and crafts
Box 300
Rochelle, Illinois
61068

CONSHOHOKEN COTTON COMPANY
Ford Bridge Road
Conshohoken, Pennsylvania
19428

DAWN
Talon American
PO Box 3823
Stamford, Connecticut
06905

EMU
Merino Wool Company
230 Fifth Avenue
New York, New York
10001

FANTACIA, INC.
415 East Beach Avenue
Inglewood, California
90302

KENDEX CORPORATION
PO Box 1909
616 Fitch Avenue
Moorpark, California
93021

LILY CRAFT PRODUCTS
B. Blumenthal & Co. Inc.
Carlstadt, New Jersey
07072

LION BRAND YARN COMPANY
1270 Broadway
New York, New York
10001

MELROSE YARN COMPANY, INC.
1305 Utica Avenue
Brooklyn, New York
11203

MERINO WOOL COMPANY
230 Fifth Avenue
New York, New York
10001

NEVADA YARN COMPANY, INC.
230 Fifth Avenue
New York, New York
10001
Attn: Consumer Inquiries –
Dept. ASB

NOMIS YARN COMPANY
146 Tosca Drive
Stoughton, Massachusetts
02072

PATONS
Susan Bates Inc.
212 Middlesex Avenue
Chester, Connecticut
06412

PLYMOUTH YARN COMPANY
PO Box 28
Bristol, Pennsylvania
19007

REYNOLDS YARNS, INC.
Box 1776
Hauppauge, New York
11788

STUDIO YARN FARMS, INC.
Dept. L
PO Box 46017
Seattle, Washington
98146

SIRDAR
Kendex Corporation
PO Box 1909
616 Fitch Avenue
Moorpark, California
93021

TALON AMERICAN
PO Box 3823
Stamford, Connecticut
06905

ULTEX YARNS, INC.
21 Adley Road
Cambridge, Massachusetts
02138

THE YARN MERCHANT
PO Box 27
Agoura Hills
CA 91301